Flourish

Twelve Guiding Principles for Out-of-School Time Professionals

Amy Brady & Lana Hailemariam

Flourish

© Copyright 2022, Amy Brady & Lana Hailemariam
All rights reserved.

All rights reserved. No portion of this book may be reproduced by mechanical, photographic or electronic process, nor may it be stored in a retrieval system, transmitted in any form or otherwise be copied for public use or private use without written permission of the copyright owners.

Printed in the United States of America

ISBN: 978-1-957058-07-8

This book is dedicated to the thousands of individuals who give tirelessly to young people during the out-of-school time hours. You are educators, planners, creators, motivators, inspirers, coaches, tear-wipers, shoe-tiers, peace-makers, celebrators, confidants, advocates, friends, mentors, role models, community connectors, leaders and difference-makers.

We see you.

Well, Hello!

So you have chosen to work with young people? Whether you are new to your role, or are a seasoned professional, we are glad you're here! You have chosen a role that can be incredibly fulfilling... and also exhausting. A role that can be joy-filled... and also difficult on some days. Here is what we know:
You will have fun. You will be inspired. And you will probably want to quit at least once!

Within these pages, you will find twelve guiding principles (or mindsets) which, when practiced with intention, will support you in bringing your absolute best to your role, even on the toughest days. We know that when you are at your best and do the work to grow and prioritize your own self-care, you will make the greatest possible impact on the youth you get to spend time with. You get to build relationships that will last a lifetime. And because those relationships can change a young person's life in big, giant ways, you are kind of a big deal. Use this book as a reminder of that, whenever you need it.

The Twelve Guiding Principles

- Open minds grow.
- We all have blind spots.
- Every feeling is valid.
- We all want to feel seen and heard.
- Every moment matters.
- Presence is a gift.
- Our WHY informs our WHAT.
- You only control the drop.
- Growth is a choice.
- You can do hard things.
- Humanity first.
- You matter.

1

Open minds grow.

Like a closed fist, a closed mind can't receive.
How open is your mind?

Wonder leads to learning.
Taking on new challenges leads to an expanded life experience.
Opening ourselves to gratitude shifts our perspective.
Curiosity leads to new solutions.
When we are open, we allow our hearts and minds to be filled.

"I love working with young people because they are so pure and welcoming. My work matters because I want young people to thrive no matter what. They are our future and they need us."

Raegan | 6 years of service

2

We all have blind spots.

To see clearly, we must see differently.
Are you committed to doing the work?

We all have parts of ourselves that we have yet to discover.
Sometimes these discoveries make us feel good about ourselves.
Many times, they don't.
But they always lead to new and impactful action.
Within the work of self-discovery lies the secret to our growth and evolution.

"Getting an opportunity to see the world through the eyes of children is a really humbling experience. I find myself inspired by their enthusiasm for life, their strength, and their resiliency."

Keliana | 5 years of service

3

Every feeling is valid.

Emotions are human.
How do you embrace emotion in yourself and others?

Our experiences inform our emotions.
Our emotions tell a story.
If we listen to that story, we more deeply connect with ourselves and others.
We demonstrate empathy.
We honor the human experience.

"I hope the work that I do has a large and lasting impact. While in my care, I hope my students feel loved, safe, and happy. I want them to become adults who make others feel loved, safe, and happy. Those are the people in the world who truly make a difference."

Sara | 15 years of service

4

We all want to feel seen and heard.

Love is necessary for human growth and development.
How do you express love?

Being fully present... this is love.
Listening deeply... this is love.
Accepting others exactly as they are (and are not)... this is love.
Feeling seen and heard is akin to feeling loved.
When we feel loved, we feel safe to grow.

"It is an honor to witness all the gifts young people bring to our lives every day. When young people feel supported, seen, and uplifted, they show up with a kindness and power that I want to see more of in the world."

| **Maya** | 7 years of service |

5

Every moment matters.

There are 1440 minutes in every day.
What will you do with them?

Consider the moments you create with everyone who crosses your path.
What will they remember about you?
How did you make them feel?
How did you bring value to every interaction?
You will only have *this* moment once.

"When I was a student in elementary school, I was bullied and often felt tossed aside by teachers because I was an 'odd child.' I want to be the adult/educator I wish I had while I was in school so that students know that it is okay to always be their authentic selves."

Randy | 5 years of service

6

Presence is a gift.

All you have right now is this moment.
How does it feel?

Feel your feet on the ground.
Take a deep breath.
Listen to your heartbeat.
You are wonderfully alive.
When you are present, you see more clearly and connect more deeply.
Your presence gives others the gift of you.

"It is important for me to create and be a safe place for our youth. I want to see them grow, finish school, and feel successful. I want to be a role model for that growth and change."

| **Tina** | 10 years of service |

7

Our WHY informs our WHAT.

Authenticity is magnetic.
Are you connected to your purpose?

When we connect *to* our heart, we connect *from* our heart.
We are intentional in our language, behavior, and energy.
We are led by what's most important to us.
We naturally inspire others.

"I hope to make an impact on the kids I work with by showing them how to be well-balanced people, how to be compassionate and caring, and also how to stand up for what they believe in. My hope is that they will use these tools as children and also as they grow into adults."

Kewhan | 11 years of service

8

You only control the drop.

For every action there is a reaction.
What ripple effect are you creating?

Life is full of choices and consequences.
When we focus on what we can control (the drop),
we are intentional in our impact.
We make a positive difference in the world around us.

"I hope that one day, one young person somewhere finds this work as equally rewarding as I do because of something I said, did, or modeled. My impact only needs to affect one person... who affects another... who affects another..."

Tammy | 28 years of service

9

Growth is a choice.

We all age, but we choose to grow.
What are you actively doing to grow both personally and professionally?

There is never a shortage of growth opportunities.
Participate in professional development.
Ask for feedback.
Learn from mistakes.
Make one change.
Each day is an opportunity to get better and do better.

"My work matters because it is in service to the most important person in the world: the child. I relish the opportunity to influence and grow young people."

| Eric | 5 years of service |

10

You can do hard things.

Every tough moment is a chance to step forward or a chance to step back.
What choice will you make?

Sometimes things will feel really hard.
Sometimes that voice in your head will scream, "I can't do this!"
Trust yourself. Listen to your heart. Be brave.
You've got this!

"I do this work because I want kids to have a space where they can feel safe and grow into themselves with the encouragement of adults who care about them. I love seeing kids make new friendships and learn new skills. They are so vulnerable, honest, and brave."

Erin | 17 years of service

11

Humanity first.

Your to-do list can wait.
How can you prioritize connection and relationships?

Spend a moment enjoying the beauty and playfulness of children.
See the good in your co-workers.
Start a conversation with a parent.
Pause. Check in. Put your hand on someone's shoulder.
These are the moments that matter.

"I do this work because I want to give back to the community I came from. I want my students to see an adult who grew up in the same neighborhoods as them, speaks the same language they do, and can relate to their background without making them feel different. It took me a long time to be proud of who I am and where I come from. I want to inspire my students to find that same pride in themselves."

Jessica | 8 years of service

12

You Matter.

There is only one you.
What is your secret sauce?

Think of the difference you make day in and day out.
You show up. You plan. You organize. You connect.
You create possibilities and deliver magic.
Celebrate yourself!
The world needs you.

"I am a product of afterschool programming and it changed my life for the better. My work matters because kids matter. Every child needs opportunities to be themselves in a space where they are not judged based on a rubric. I love the opportunity to see kids progress and reach a goal; their joy and happiness when they accomplish something makes all the long days and hard work pay off."

Sydney | 17 years of service

We would like to give a huge shout out to the Denver OST community. We have met so many incredible humans in our work who inspire us every single day. Twelve of these many individuals appear on the pages of this book. To these real people, doing the real work: You have let us push you and challenge you. You have been willing to try new things and see new perspectives. You have shared your stories with us, and have listened with so much heart when we have shared ours. You have shown up for us time and time again. We are continuously moved, grateful and humbled.

A special thanks to the Denver Office of Children's Affairs and the Denver Afterschool Alliance for embracing and elevating our work. Thank you for trusting us.

And, finally, to our young people: *You are the WHY.*

open minds grow

www.ingramcontent.com/pod-product-compliance
Lightning Source LLC
Chambersburg PA
CBHW040002290426
43673CB00078B/335